NATIONAL GEOGRAPHIC

D0100736

Making Tortillas

Michelle Freeman

Jordan and I are going to make tortillas.
We need all of these things.

spatula
skillet
paper towel
warm water
flour
rolling pin

First, Jordan puts the flour, salt,
and baking powder in a bowl.
I stir them together.
Then, we add the oil and water.
We stir it to make a dough.

I press and roll the dough.
This makes the dough smooth and stretch
Then, we shape the dough into balls.

I flatten the balls with a rolling pin.
Tortillas are round and flat.

Mom cooks the tortillas.
Then, she puts them on a paper towel to drain.

We all helped make the tortillas.
We all help eat the tortillas, too.